FOOTBALL SKILLS

CLIVE GIFFORD

KINGFISHER

Contents

The beautiful game

Brazilian footballing legend Pele once described football as 'the beautiful game'. Matches can be exciting and dramatic. They can contain moments of bravery, controversy, great skill and action. Two teams of players battle to keep possession of the ball, attack their opponents' end of the pitch and try to score a goal.

Goals win games, but teams need to defend to stop goals being scored against them and to win the ball back. When in possession of the ball, players can use any part of their body except the hands and arms to control and move the ball or pass it to a teammate.

Germany's Sylvia Arnold (right) challenges the USA's Crystal Dunn during an international match. The very best players get the chance to represent their country at different tournaments.

"Football is simple, but the hardest thing there is, is to play simple football."

Johan Cruyff

Children in the city of Niamey in Niger use a street as a makeshift pitch. Because football is a simple game that needs little equipment, millions of people in all parts of the world play casual games every day.

Many ancient civilizations, including the Egyptians and the Chinese, played games in which players kicked a ball. Association football (the modern version of the game) has its historic home in England, however, where the first rules were drawn up in the 19th century. Since then, football has been exported all over the world to become the most popular team sport on the planet.

Wayne Rooney scores with a spectacular overhead kick during a match between his club, Manchester United, and local rivals Manchester City.

Players battle it out in a street football match during the 18th century. Football developed from these unruly mob football games into a global sport.

Players celebrate a goal scored by one of their teammates. Although the player may have conjured up a moment of magic to score, teamwork from the other players on his team created the opportunity to strike.

The pitch

The pitch is where heroes are made, goals are scored and matches won and lost. Unlike most other sports, a football pitch can vary in size. A full-sized pitch is 90–120m long and up to 90m wide. Pitches for professional matches are usually covered with grass, although artificial pitches are found in some stadia.

Top footballers often look exhausted at the end of a match – players may have to run 10–12km during a game. Play stops only if the referee blows the whistle for a foul or other infringement, or if the ball leaves the pitch.

This goalkeeper takes a goal kick from the front of her goal area. Goal kicks are awarded when the ball crosses the goal line and it was touched last by an attacking player. If a defending player touches the ball last, a corner is awarded.

A defender trips and fouls an attacker inside the penalty area. A serious foul, which prevents a possible goalscoring chance, results in a penalty awarded to the attacking team (see page 46).

Goal line

Goal area

Goalkeepers are the only players who can touch the ball with their hands and arms, but they must be inside their own penalty area. This keeper has handled the ball outside his area and the opposing team will be awarded a free kick (see page 44).

The football stays in play even when part of it crosses a sideline or goal line.

The football has to completely cross a line to go out of play. If it leaves the side of the pitch, then the game will be restarted with a throw-in (see page 42).

An attacking player blasts a free kick past a wall of defensive players and at the goal. A full-sized goal is made up of a net fitted to two posts and a crossbar. The goal measures 7.32m wide and 2.44m high.

Penalty area

Centre circle

Penalty spot

Centre spot

Halfway line

Sideline

Each half of the game is started with one team taking a kick-off from the middle of the centre circle. The first touch must move the ball into the opponent's half and the opposition team must stay outside the centre circle until it is made. Kick-offs are also used to restart the game after a goal.

Corner quadrant

A player takes a corner, aiming to cross the ball into the other team's penalty area for his teammates to try and score. The ball must be played from inside the small corner quadrant.

PROFESSIONAL: football in which the players are paid a full-time wage to play

Football terms

Preparing to play

Leaping high to head a ball one minute and sprinting hard or lunging for the ball the next – football puts your body under a lot of strain throughout a match. You should prepare your body and mind for the effort by performing a good warm-up and muscle-stretching routine beforehand.

Your footwear is by far the most important part of your equipment. Ignore boots advertised by star players in favour of ones that best fit your feet, feel comfortable and offer good support around your ankle. Many good boots feature soft leather uppers so that your foot can 'feel' the ball. Clean and dry your boots after each game so they will last for many matches.

These football boots feature screw-in studs to provide plenty of grip on a soft, wet pitch. Make sure all studs are tightened before play. Other types of boot have moulded pimples for use on dry, hard ground and artificial pitches.

Tie your boot laces securely in a double knot, making sure the lace ends do not trail on the ground.

A coach shows players how to stretch the hamstring muscles at the backs of their legs. All stretches should be performed smoothly. Never jerk or bounce into a stretch or perform them half-heartedly.

Players jog on the spot and perform high knee lifts, raising their knees so that their upper thighs are parallel to the ground. Tracksuits may be worn to stay warm before a game.

A long-haired footballer ties her hair back before beginning a training session. Players must also remove any jewellery before they start playing a match.

If you get a few minutes on the pitch before a game, check out wind and weather conditions, and make some passes with teammates to get a feel for the speed of the pitch.

⚽ *PRO TIPS* ⚽

Warming up can involve jogging and other activities that raise your heart rate and get your blood pumping faster around your body. Stretching muscles helps prevent small muscle niggles or more serious tears and injuries, and improves your flexibility, too. Ask your coach to take you through a thorough stretching routine.

Shinpads protect the bony front parts of your lower legs from painful kicks during tackling. Many also have padding around the ankle and heel area for added protection. Socks are pulled up over the shinpads and secured with ties.

"Failure to prepare. Prepare to fail."

Roy Keane, ex-Manchester United and Ireland midfielder

FLEXIBILITY: the amount you can move your joints and body parts

Football terms

First touch

The ball will zip, fly and bounce towards you at a great variety of speeds, heights and angles during a game. How quickly, smoothly and accurately you are able to control it with your first touch will determine how successful your next move is. You can use any part of your body, apart from your hands and arms, to control the ball. You can either cushion the ball's speed or use its pace to make a short pass or run with the ball.

Much of the time, you will want to slow the ball down on arrival so that you can get it under control near your feet in order to run, pass or shoot. Players cushion the ball by withdrawing the body part that connects with the ball as it arrives. By moving their foot, thigh or chest along the same path as the ball's, they can slow its pace so that it does not bounce out of their control.

A player controls a high ball using his chest. As the ball arrives, he leans back to cushion the ball's impact. His feet have a wide stance and his arms are out to help him balance. The ball should drop gently in front of his feet, ready to be controlled on the ground.

Practise cushioning the ball with the side and instep (where the laces are) of both feet. A player who can control the ball equally well with both feet offers a greater threat.

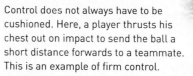

PRO TIPS

Control does not always have to be cushioned. Here, a player thrusts his chest out on impact to send the ball a short distance forwards to a teammate. This is an example of firm control.

While most headers (see page 18) use firm control, a cushioned header will bring the ball down or can be used to make a short pass to a nearby teammate. The secret is to draw your head back as the ball arrives to kill much of its pace.

To cushion a falling ball with the top of your thigh, raise your upper leg so that it is almost parallel with the ground. As the ball arrives, drop your knee and pull your leg back and down so that the ball is cushioned and drops in front of you.

The side of the foot can be used to control a bouncing ball or one that is rolling across the ground. This player has turned her receiving foot to present the inside of the boot to the ball. This is drawn back as the ball arrives.

A good first touch only comes with a lot of practice. Work on your first touch and ball control whenever you can. Get a friend to pass the ball to you at different heights and speeds, or use a wall to bounce the ball off if on your own. Concentrate on being balanced and watching the ball, so that you can bring it under control as quickly as possible.

> "When your first touch is good, it always gives you time to see the next situation."
>
> *Rafael van der Vaart, Dutch attacking midfielder*

To outwit an opponent, this player has let a pass run across in front of his body rather than controlling the ball straight away. He turns sharply to move in the direction of the ball's path, using its pace to leave the opponent behind.

Football terms   **CUSHIONING**: slowing the path of the ball using a part of the body

Passing

Passing moves the ball between teammates and slick, accurate passing can propel the ball around the pitch far faster than by running with it. A team that passes well is likely to split defences and create goalscoring opportunities. Passes can vary in force and distance, from short flicks to long passes that cross the pitch. They can also be made with different parts of your feet.

You can use the outside of your foot to make a short flick pass by twisting your foot at the ankle sharply. This is a useful, quick pass to a teammate standing a short distance away.

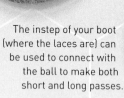

The instep of your boot (where the laces are) can be used to connect with the ball to make both short and long passes.

1

To make a sidefoot pass, place your non-kicking foot to the side of the ball and turn your ankle so that the inside of your kicking foot faces the ball.

2

Swing your leg forwards through the ball. Aim to make contact with the centre of the ball – this keeps it low for your teammate to control easily.

3

As the ball moves away, your foot should follow through in the direction the ball is heading. Try to keep your body over the ball during the pass.

With a lot of practice, you will be able to judge how much force you need to strike the ball to make a pass. This is known as the weight of the pass. Too much weight, and the pass will be difficult to control. Too little weight, and it might not reach your teammate. You can adjust the weight of your pass by taking your kicking foot back a longer or shorter distance and striking the ball with more or less force.

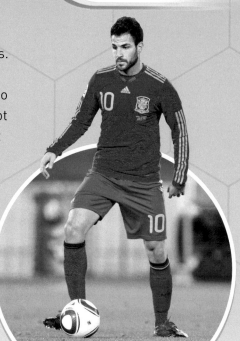

Masterclass

Cesc Fabregas

The gifted midfielder is a renowned passer of the ball with both feet, able to play short passes to keep possession or play a timely attacking ball to create a goal. It was Fabregas's pinpoint pass to teammate Andrés Iniesta that produced the winning goal for Spain in the 2010 World Cup final against the Netherlands.

Four players practise their short passing in a 2 v 2 game played inside a small, coned-off area. One pair tries to make as many passes as possible without the other pair intercepting a pass or the ball travelling out of the area.

"If you want to make it as a footballer, you probably need to be practising simple side foot passing every single day."

Gary Neville, ex-Manchester United and England defender

Pass placement is crucial. This player has aimed the ball some distance ahead of his teammate so that he can sprint onto the ball and behind the opposition player. Learning when to make a pass and the best place to aim the ball only comes with practice and experience.

INTERCEPTING: when one team makes a pass but an opponent gains control of the ball

Football terms

To make an instep drive, plant your non-kicking foot beside the ball and keep your body weight over the ball as you swing your kicking foot back.

Point your kicking foot down as you swing forwards. Aim to strike the centre of the ball with your boot laces.

Keeping your eyes on the ball throughout, let your kicking leg follow through smoothly. The ball should fly away towards its target.

Advanced passing

Apart from building a large range of passes to use, the most crucial element of developing your passing skills is to learn to pass well with both feet. Every footballer starts out with a weaker foot. The secret is to work extra hard on that foot to bring it up to the level of your strongest. A footballer who favours one foot is far easier to play against because defenders know their opponent can only play the ball on one side of his or her body.

A lofted drive relies on similar technique to a regular instep drive. You create the extra height on the ball by leaning back a little as you strike the bottom half of the ball with your instep.

To make a chip pass, use a short, stabbing movement of your instep down on the bottom of the ball.

Your boot acts like a wedge. The ball should rise sharply into the air, with little follow through.

Much of the time you will want to keep the ball low so that it speeds across the pitch surface, but there are times when you want to send the ball higher. A chip pass can send the ball steeply up and over an opponent. A lofted drive is a strong strike of the ball used for making crosses into the opponent's penalty area or to clear the ball a long way out of your own penalty area.

This attacker in white places his body between the ball and an opponent to protect the ball before playing it to a teammate.

★ *Masterclass* ★

Steven Gerrard

Liverpool and England midfielder Steven Gerrard plays a trademark long pass to launch an attack. Gerrard is highly skilled at picking out teammates with both long- and short-range passes. He also uses the instep drive as a powerful shooting weapon to score many goals from outside the penalty area.

Try not to dawdle on the ball or be too obvious about where your pass is going to go. Play with your head up and try to make accurate passes to avoid the risk of interception.

PRO TIPS

The greater your range of passes, the more options you will have when on the ball. Choosing when to use a particular pass is even more crucial. Think safety first when playing the ball out of your defensive third of the pitch and never consider it a failure if you choose to pass sideways or back when attacking. Keeping possession is important.

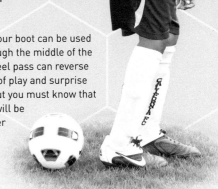

The back of your boot can be used to strike through the middle of the ball. A backheel pass can reverse the direction of play and surprise opponents, but you must know that a teammate will be there to gather the ball.

"Some teams can't or don't pass the ball. What are you playing for? What's the point?"

Xavi, Spain and Barcelona midfielder

Football terms   **CROSS:** a pass sent from a wide position into the penalty area

Heading

Around one in five goals is scored with a header, but heading isn't just used in attack. It is a vital part of defensive play and with the ball bouncing high off firm ground, headers can be used all over the pitch by every player. Even goalkeepers use headers to clear a high ball when they are outside their penalty area.

Headers are often directed downwards, towards a teammate's feet or aimed at goal. In these cases, players try to get their head over the ball and aim to connect just above the middle of the ball. When you want elevation on the ball, for example to clear the ball up and over opponents, aim for just below the middle of the ball.

Get into line with the direction of the ball, watch it carefully and spring upwards, swinging your arms forwards to help you leap high.

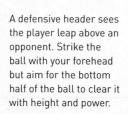

A defensive header sees the player leap above an opponent. Strike the ball with your forehead but aim for the bottom half of the ball to clear it with height and power.

Rising above the ball, this attacker has managed to direct his header downwards towards the bottom corner of the goal, making it very hard for the goalkeeper to react in time.

This player has made a glancing header by flicking her head to one side, as she makes contact, to deflect the path of the ball slightly towards a teammate.

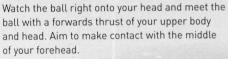

Watch the ball right onto your head and meet the ball with a forwards thrust of your upper body and head. Aim to make contact with the middle of your forehead.

Keep your neck muscles firm as you connect to push the ball away strongly. Bend your knees to help cushion your landing.

The diving header is one of the most spectacular of all moves in football. This player has launched himself to get to the ball ahead of defenders and has glanced it towards goal.

★ *Masterclass* ★

Tim Cahill

Tim Cahill times his jump to head the ball perfectly. Relatively short for a professional footballer, at 1.78m, the Australian midfielder is a masterful header of the ball both in defence and in attack. His bravery and powerful spring usually see him get to the ball ahead of opponents.

PENALTY AREA: the rectangular area surrounding each goal

Football terms

Finding space

Space gives players time and opportunity to control the ball and develop their team's attack. Pockets of space appear all over the pitch and good players learn to spot the most attractive spaces to move into. Moving into these spaces can stretch the other team or create an overload – an area of the pitch where the attacking team has more players than the defending side.

These attackers in white are playing a one-two move. The first attacker (the player nearest to us) plays a short pass to his teammate, before sprinting quickly into space behind the defender in order to receive a return pass.

Moving into space is not just a question of spotting a promising free area of the pitch, but also of timing your move. Try to stay aware of where the ball and other players are and look to time your run to stay onside (see page 48). As soon as you make a pass, make sure you move straight away and look for another good position to receive the ball.

The attacker on the right has spotted her teammate making a well-timed diagonal run into space. With an accurate pass, she can send the ball over the opposition player so that her teammate is behind the defence.

Timing your run to move onto the ball in space behind a defence is an especially good move. One player makes an overlapping run outside a defender and down the edge of the pitch. His teammate plays the ball in front of him so that he can run onto it, behind the opposition defence.

Getting into space often means getting free of an opponent marking you. You should never jog aimlessly from place to place. Instead, make your runs sharp, accurate and decisive. You can use changes of pace to get free of your marker as well as feints, where you drop your shoulder and pretend to head one way, before pushing off hard from one foot and sprinting in a different direction.

1

The player in white is trying to get free from her marker. She feints a move to her left by taking a large step in that direction – the defender follows.

As soon as she plants her left foot, she uses it to push off and move quickly to her right. The defender has been caught out by this move and has been left behind.

2

If you make a run into space but do not receive the ball and the game moves on, do not dawdle. Instead, look for other places to move into as soon as you can.

PRO TIPS

★ Masterclass ★

Xavi
Playing with his head up as usual, the gifted Spanish midfielder is a master at seeking out space both to move into to receive a pass and to aim passes for teammates. Xavi made more passes than any player at the 2010 World Cup (669 in total) and is a crucial part of what makes his club side, Barcelona, one of the most successful teams in the world.

Playing small-sided games and drills that emphasize quick passing and movement will help to improve your ability to play with your head up, spot space and move into it quickly and decisively.

Football terms   **FEINT**: using a fake move of the body to send an opponent the wrong way

Shielding and dribbling

The ball will often arrive when an opponent is very close to you. You can protect possession by getting your body between the opponent and the ball. This technique is called shielding. Running with the ball under close control is known as dribbling. It can be a useful technique to beat defenders when attacking.

Dribbling carries the risk of losing the ball, so it is best attempted as an attacking move only when a good pass is not available. Try to use both feet to nudge and push the ball, keeping it a little ahead of you, but not too far. For dribbling to be successful in a match, it should be performed quickly or with sudden changes of pace and direction.

Deception, fakes and swerves are all part of becoming a successful dribbler. This dribbler in white fakes a move to her right, which the defender follows.

The defender lunges in the direction she believes the dribbler is heading. At the same time, the dribbler brings her left foot around the ball to move it to her left.

With the ball under control, the dribbler moves sharply away to her left. The defender is unbalanced and unable to regain a good defensive position before the dribbler passes her.

When shielding the ball you should be aware of where your opponent is at all times. Stay on the balls of your feet so that you can move as the opponent moves, and keep your body and arms out to make as big a shield as possible. Keep the ball under control and think about your next move, whether this is a sharp turn or a pass to a teammate.

You can stand your ground as you shield the ball, but if you back into your opponent or cause an obstruction, then you commit a foul.

★ *Masterclass* ★

Lionel Messi
Argentinian maestro Lionel Messi shields the ball from the Greek defender, Sokratis Papastathopoulos, during a 2010 World Cup game. Messi is relatively small and light, but with excellent balance, awareness, ball control and movement, he is able to keep possession of the ball and dribble skilfully past defenders.

If you cannot turn past a defender, keep the ball shielded and look for a short lay-off pass to a teammate to the side or behind you.

To complete a stepover, bring one foot across the ball as if it were to connect with the ball.

Instead of connecting, lift your foot over the ball and plant it to one side.

You can then use your other foot to tap the ball in the other direction, confusing a defender.

Alternatively, you can perform another stepover with the other foot.

OBSTRUCTION: blocking an opponent from reaching the ball

Football terms

A player works on his close control skills by dribbling through a slalom of poles with the ball under close control. A good way to learn many new moves is to attempt them at walking pace first, and gradually build up speed as you improve.

In training

While you should practise your individual skills whenever you can, training sessions are where you can practise with others under the eye of your coach. He or she can give you direct tuition on key techniques while you work with teammates in fun and challenging drills and games, and learn set-piece plays, such as special corner or free-kick moves.

A coach works with players, showing the defenders good positions to take up when defending a corner. Good coaches organize varied and interesting sessions with different drills and games to challenge you and improve your skills.

Attending regular football training sessions will improve your physical fitness and stamina and allow you to practise passing, moving, attacking and defending techniques with other players in realistic game situations. Working on your core individual skills in between training sessions will help to improve your technique and ability rapidly.

Training can be thirsty work, so make sure you take small, regular sips from a water bottle during breaks in training.

Approach training as you would a match, by warming up and stretching thoroughly and then committing yourself to every part of the training session. Concentrate on each drill and always listen to your coach. If you do not understand a point, ask your coach to explain it to you.

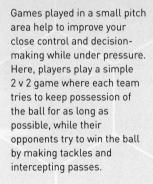

This attacker is practising his shooting while the keeper is practising his diving saves.

Games played in a small pitch area help to improve your close control and decision-making while under pressure. Here, players play a simple 2 v 2 game where each team tries to keep possession of the ball for as long as possible, while their opponents try to win the ball by making tackles and intercepting passes.

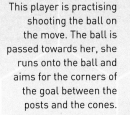

This player is practising shooting the ball on the move. The ball is passed towards her, she runs onto the ball and aims for the corners of the goal between the posts and the cones.

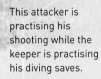

Football terms   **SET PIECE:** a restart move such as a free kick, corner or throw-in

Volleys and swerves

A volley is a strike of the ball while it is in the air. It can be powerful if performed well, but it is one of the trickiest skills to master. Softer volleys can be made to cushion a short pass to a teammate or to steer the ball into an open goal to score.

To make a side volley, lean away from the ball a little as you move your arms out and swing your leg up and round at the hip.

To make a front-on volley, swing your kicking leg back and forwards, holding your arms out for balance.

Keeping your head over the ball, point your foot down before striking the ball with your boot instep.

Swing your leg to follow through in the direction of the target.

Get your foot over the ball so that your instep makes contact with its top half if you want to keep the ball down, or just below the middle if you are making a defensive clearance.

Volleys are used when there is little time to get the ball down and control it. This occurs both in attack and defence when you need to make a fast clearance. The secret with all volleys is to watch the ball carefully and to time your leg swing with the incoming ball's speed and direction.

To make an overhead kick, jump back off one leg and swing your other leg up and over to strike the ball with your instep at the highest point. Try to relax as you fall and roll on your shoulders to absorb the impact.

"Make sure your non-kicking foot is firmly planted. If it isn't, you could be off balance."

Alfred Galustian, technical adviser to the English Premier League

As you follow through, look to get your foot on the ground and regain your balance as quickly as possible.

To strike an inside swerve with your right foot, plant your left foot away from the ball. Use the inside of your foot to strike the righthand side of the back of the ball. Aim for a straight follow through of your leg to send the ball curving to the left.

★ Masterclass ★

Samir Nasri

This dynamic French midfielder is a master at bending the ball, either to hit a curling pass to a teammate or to unleash a wicked, swerving shot on goal. After playing more than 120 times for French club Marseille, Nasri enjoyed three seasons at Arsenal before moving to Manchester City for £25 million.

Hitting across the back and one side of the ball with a specific part of your boot can put spin on the ball, making it swerve through the air. This can be useful not just to bend the ball round a defensive wall during a free kick, but also to cross the ball into the penalty area on a path curving towards or away from the goal.

Remember that swerving the ball down the sideline may get it past an opponent, but if the whole of the ball crosses the sideline while in the air, the other team will get a throw-in.

PRO TIPS

To hit an outside swerve, use the outside of your right boot to strike across the back and left side of the ball. Your kicking foot should swing up and across your body as the ball curves to the right.

SWERVE: to bend the path of the ball

Football terms

An attacking team will look to get a player into a position from which they can score. Sometimes, a burst of individual brilliance can result in a goal. However, goals are usually a team effort with players working together to create space for teammates or to release another attacker with a through ball behind the defence.

The player on the ball faces a crowded penalty area. His teammates look to make diagonal attacking runs, staying onside until the ball is played.

The attacker to the left makes a run to one side, drawing his defender with him and creating space for the attacker on the ball to play a through ball into the gap.

Attacking

Good teams and players try to use all parts of the pitch to launch and develop attacks. By passing the ball from the centre of the pitch out wide, for example, you can look to cross the ball into the penalty area. This can stretch the opposing team's defence, potentially creating gaps for players to run into.

You can sometimes beat an opponent without dribbling by pushing the ball past them and sprinting hard to get the ball back under control. This can work best down the sidelines of the pitch when there is no covering defender nearby.

3

The other attacker can then run behind his marker into the space to receive the pass and shoot at goal.

★ *Masterclass* ★

Mesut Özil

Mesut Özil plays a defence-splitting pass during Germany's 4-0 win over Australia at the 2010 World Cup. Özil is an exciting young attacking midfielder with a great eye for through balls, pinpoint crosses from wide positions or sudden bursts through opposing defences. After starring at the World Cup, Özil moved from Werder Bremen to Spanish club Real Madrid.

This attacker has run towards goal after a teammate has shot. As a result, she is in a great position to pounce on a mistake by the goalkeeper and tap the ball into the net.

The attacker on the ball has spotted plenty of space behind the opposition defence. He can play the ball diagonally across the pitch for his teammate on the far side to run onto.

Scoring goals

Scoring goals is a joy but also a great skill. It calls for sharp reactions, cool decision making and great awareness of the game going on around you. While strikers may get more chances to score on average, all outfield players should work on their shooting because defenders and midfielders often get opportunities to score in close matches.

Different situations demand different types of shot, but try not to over-hit the ball, even with longer-distance strikes on goal, and make sure your shot is on target. Work hard to perfect your shooting with both feet. This will give you more opportunity to strike and stops a defender from forcing you onto your weaker foot.

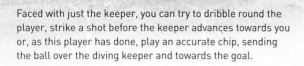
Faced with just the keeper, you can try to dribble round the player, strike a shot before the keeper advances towards you or, as this player has done, play an accurate chip, sending the ball over the diving keeper and towards the goal.

★ Masterclass ★

Birgit Prinz

Birgit Prinz celebrates scoring a goal for her team, Frankfurt FFC. The German goal machine has scored more than 120 times for her country, more than 200 times for her club and is the all-time leading scorer at the Women's World Cup with 14 goals. She has also been FIFA World Player of the Year three times.

Do not get upset if you fail to score. Top players miss chances but are mentally strong. Try to put mistakes out of your mind and get back into the game straight away.

PRO TIPS

This player's first attempt on goal rebounded off a defender, but by following up his own shot quickly he gets to the ball first. Close to goal, he opts for placement over power by making a sidefoot pass into the net.

If you are in a good shooting position, within your shooting range and have a clear sight of goal, do not hesitate – shoot! Football is a fast-moving sport and, within a second, defenders will close you down. Pick the type of shot you want to make, aim away from the keeper and try to keep your body over the ball to keep the shot low.

There are lots of different drills you can use to work on your shooting skills. Here, one player controls the ball with her back to goal.

Quick reactions and awareness close to goal can make the difference. The player on the left could shoot the ball to the goalkeeper's left or play in a teammate who is in a better position to score.

Once the ball is under control, she must turn quickly and fire off an accurate shot past the goalkeeper.

Football terms | OUTFIELD PLAYER: any footballer in a team except the goalkeeper

Defending

Defending is a task for every player on a team, not just the goalkeeper and defenders. A well-organized team, with all players working hard for each other, denies the opposing team time and space to build good attacks. When defending, you have two aims – to prevent goalscoring chances being created and to regain possession of the ball for your side.

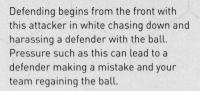

Defending begins from the front with this attacker in white chasing down and harassing a defender with the ball. Pressure such as this can lead to a defender making a mistake and your team regaining the ball.

In some teams, each defender is instructed by their coach to guard an area of the pitch, a technique known as zonal marking. Most junior teams prefer man-marking, where each defender and some midfielders are responsible for staying close to a particular opponent. They stay close as their opponents move to deny them time and space to receive the ball.

This marker in yellow stays sharp and moves as his opponent moves, staying on the balls of his feet so he can move quickly in any direction. He stays goalside of his opponent at all times.

As an opponent shoots, the defender gets his body and legs in the way to block the ball. When you block a shot, try to keep your hands close to your body to avoid a handball offence.

This defender has jockeyed his opponent, delaying his movement towards goal as a teammate arrives to provide defensive cover. Once his teammate is in support, the defender may choose to challenge for the ball.

Jockeying is the skill of closing down an opponent and delaying their progress in attack. Get into a good, defensive stance around 1–2m in front of your opponent with your knees bent, eyes on the ball, and try to keep your distance by retreating in a zig-zag pattern. If you can, try to direct your opponent away from goal.

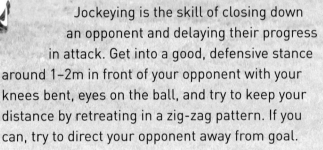

This defender in yellow is under pressure from two attackers. She has no choice but to put the ball out of play over the sideline, giving her time to get back into position.

Clearing the ball can relieve pressure on your team. If you have time on the ball, look to make an accurate pass to a teammate in plenty of space. If time is short, look to strike the ball upfield.

"Stay on your feet, don't dive in – defending is all about timing."

Rio Ferdinand, Manchester United and England defender

Football terms   GOALSIDE: placing your body in between the goal and the ball or an opponent

Challenging for the ball

The aim of challenging for the ball is to win back possession for your team. This might not always be possible, but any challenge should at least try to slow down an opponent's attack. An ideal challenge sees you move away with the ball under your control, ready to turn defence into attack.

This defender has used his pace to get ahead of an opponent with the ball. Shoulder charging an opponent is illegal but some contact between the players' shoulders is acceptable.

★ Masterclass ★

Maicon

Brazilian defender Maicon times a sliding tackle perfectly to dispossess USA midfielder DaMarcus Beasley. Strong and decisive when challenging for the ball, Maicon looks to regain possession and turn defence into attack whenever possible. A superb defender for his club side, Inter Milan, he was voted UEFA Club Defender of the Year in 2010.

Try to make a challenge when you have teammates providing cover between you and your goal. Sometimes, a defender can race in and intercept the ball without tackling. If you do have to make a challenge, try to stay on your feet and make sure you connect with the ball rather than your opponent.

The defender in yellow looks to make a front block tackle. She establishes a firm low base with a strong stance and her standing leg bent slightly at the knee. Her eyes watch the ball rather than the player as she times her challenge.

She uses the inside of her boot to make a strong strike through the middle of the ball, leaning into the challenge as impact occurs. With all her body weight in the tackle, the ball spills free and she reacts quickly to get it under control.

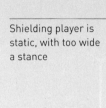

Shielding player is static, with too wide a stance

Defender pokes ball away with the toe of his boot

Block tackles see you put your body weight into a firm strike of the ball with the inside of your foot. The ball can sometimes get wedged between your foot and your opponent's. In this situation, the first to flick or roll the ball up and over the other's foot often gains possession of the ball.

When an opponent shields the ball from you, look for opportunities to win possession, pressure your opponent into a mistake or to move the ball out of your opponent's control – but be careful not to give away a foul. This defender has managed to poke his foot between the attacker's legs and nudge the ball away.

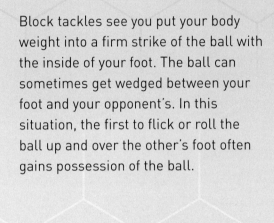

A block tackle can be made from the side using a similar technique to the front block. Time your approach, face your opponent and bend your standing leg at the knee before striking the ball firmly with the inside of your boot.

Goalkeeping

Good goalkeeping is as much about awareness and positioning as about spectacular saves. As a goalkeeper, you are your team's defensive leader. You are responsible for organizing the team at set pieces, such as corners and free kicks, and when an opposing team breaks with the ball. You should also pass on advice and instructions to teammates, making them clear and loud.

This keeper is in a good ready position with his hands up and out, his head level and his eyes focused on the ball and play ahead of him.

Goalkeeping starts from the ready position where you are balanced with your weight equally on the balls of both feet and your knees slightly bent. From this position you can move easily and quickly in any direction, reacting to move in line with the ball to block a shot, jump quickly towards a deflection, gather the ball in cleanly or sprint forwards to kick the ball clear.

Stay alert for a back pass from a teammate. If headed back, you can catch the ball, but if it is kicked you cannot pick it up. If under pressure, think safety first and kick the ball out of play.

PRO TIPS

To gather a ball rolling along or just above the ground, get in line with the ball's path, drop down onto one knee and scoop the ball up to your chest. Your leg and body act as a barrier behind your hands.

To catch a high ball, leap up from one foot and stretch up with your arms. Aim to catch it in front of you, spreading your hands around the back and sides of the ball.

Overarm throws are used to bowl the ball out quickly over medium to long distances. With a wide, side-on stance for balance, bring your throwing arm forwards over your head and release the ball. Your other arm should point to your intended target.

★ *Masterclass* ★

Gianluigi Buffon

The Italian goalkeeper keeps his eye on the ball as he stretches to deflect a shot around his post. Buffon became the world's most expensive goalkeeper when he transferred from Parma to Juventus for £32.6 million in 2001. His calmness under pressure and expert positioning allow him to stop many attacks.

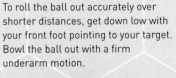

To roll the ball out accurately over shorter distances, get down low with your front foot pointing to your target. Bowl the ball out with a firm underarm motion.

If you think you cannot catch a high ball cleanly, you can punch it clear with two hands. Aim to punch through the back of the ball to send it forwards and up, out of your penalty area.

To catch a ball around waist height, scoop the ball into your body. Cushion its arrival by bending and folding your body around the ball.

To perform a drop kick, hold the ball out in front of you, drop it and aim to hit the ball with the instep of your boot just before it reaches the ground.

Advanced goalkeeping

Sometimes, good positioning is not enough and an opposing attacker bursts through on goal. These are the moments when a goalkeeper needs bravery, explosive agility and good technique to make a crucial save. In these situations, keepers must be quick and decisive. If they fail to get to the ball first and collide with or trip an attacker they will give away a penalty and may be shown a red card.

Diving at the feet of an opponent can be a scary experience, so practise it gently in training to build your confidence. In a game situation, once you decide to go to ground, attack the ball. Keep your eyes on the ball, not the opponent, and try to spread yourself, creating a long barrier across the ground. Get your hands on the ball and wrap your body around it for added protection.

If you spot the flight of a shot heading to one side of you, you may be forced to make a diving save. Try to take short, very quick steps in that direction and start bending your knee nearest that side.

Transfer your body weight over your bent knee and push off hard from that foot to spring up and across your goal. Keep your eyes on the ball and the path it is travelling on.

With a goalkeeper staying on his line, an attacker with the ball has the whole of the goal to aim at. The keeper will struggle if an attacker hits a shot into the corners.

Narrowing the angle is a key positioning technique to reduce the amount of the goal an opponent with the ball can shoot at. You need to come out of your goal, but positioned along an imaginary line running from the ball to the centre of your goal.

All goalkeepers have a stronger and weaker side and saves they prefer. Work hard on your weaker side and least favourite saves to bring them up to the level of your other skills.

PRO TIPS

This keeper has come off his line to narrow the angle and has spread his body and arms to look as big as possible. Attackers can see far less of the goal, and, as a result, they may hit a shot wide.

As you dive, stretch both of your arms out and a little in front of you, so you can watch the ball right into your hands. Your hands should be nicely spread, but close enough together to be ready to grasp the sides and back of the ball.

With the ball caught, gather it into your body and prepare for landing. Try to land on your side, using it as a buffer or cushion when you hit the ground to stop the ball jarring out of your grip.

Laws of the game

The rules of football are enforced on the pitch by the referee and two assistants, who communicate with the referee using flag signals. The referee must decide whether a foul has been committed and judge which team touched the ball last when awarding corners, throw-ins and goal kicks. Never argue with a referee's call – the referee's decision is final.

Referees can discipline individual players by showing a yellow card for a range of offences, including fouls, arguing with the referee or preventing the restart of play. More severe offences result in a red card. In this case, the offending player leaves the pitch and his or her team must continue with one fewer player.

The attacker in white has been fouled by his opponent, but has managed to keep hold of the ball and is in a good attacking position. Instead of stopping play and awarding a free kick, the referee lets the attacker continue and puts both of his arms out in front to signal that he is playing advantage.

With his team in the lead, this goalkeeper has held on to the ball for longer than 10 seconds. He is guilty of delaying the restart of play – known as timewasting – and the referee cautions him by showing a yellow card. If a player is shown two yellow cards in a match, then he or she is automatically shown a red card and must leave the pitch.

Pretending to be fouled is known as simulation. In this case, the referee is playing advantage as the diving player has not been fouled. He can also award a free kick to the opposition.

Throw-in

Substitution being made

Offside

A player is offside if, as the ball is played by a teammate, they are nearer to the opposition's goal line than both the ball and the second-last opponent. You cannot be offside if you receive the ball directly from a throw-in, corner or goal kick. If you are offside, the referee will award an indirect free kick to the other team.

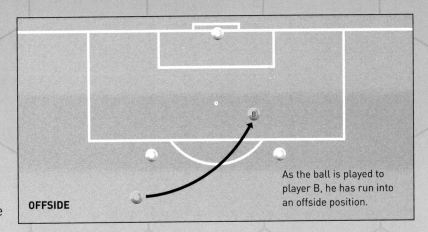

OFFSIDE

As the ball is played to player B, he has run into an offside position.

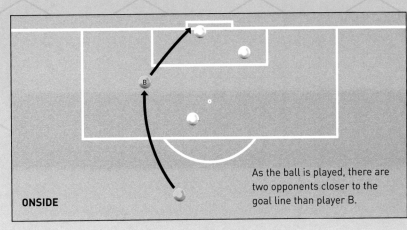

ONSIDE

As the ball is played, there are two opponents closer to the goal line than player B.

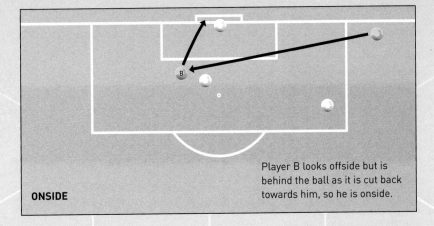

ONSIDE

Player B looks offside but is behind the ball as it is cut back towards him, so he is onside.

Penalty

Indirect free kick

Red card

Corner

Goal kick

Football terms   **ADVANTAGE:** when a referee lets play continue after a law has been broken

Throw-ins are given when the ball crosses the pitch's sideline. A player must keep two hands on the ball during the throw and his feet must be on or behind the sideline. To make a longer throw, you can take several steps to build momentum before launching the ball. Arch your back and whip your arms and body forwards, releasing the ball with a flick of your fingers.

For a throw-in, take your arms back over your head with your hands spread around the back and sides of the ball, and keep both feet on the ground.

Whip your upper body forwards as your arms travel over your head. Release the ball with a flick of your wrists and fingers to help direct the ball.

This player commits a foul throw because he has stepped over the sideline. Other causes of a foul throw are lifting one foot off the ground and not bringing the ball back over your head.

Restarting play

Play stops for a number of reasons — for example, if the ball leaves the playing area across a goal line or sideline, or if the referee halts the game for an injury or foul. The match is restarted in several ways. These are great opportunities for your team to build attacks. For this reason, moves involving corners and throw-ins are often part of training for a team.

Successful throw-ins rely on cooperation between teammates to secure possession. Here, this throw-in decoy move sees one teammate sprint towards the thrower, drawing the defender with him. This creates space behind for the other attacker to run into and receive the ball from the throw.

Most corners are aimed at the front of the goal area for attackers to try to head at the goal. The corner taker must beat the first defender, who is often placed in front of the near goalpost. Good corner takers aim to put plenty of pace on the ball, as the slightest deflection can propel the ball towards the goal.

By bending the ball (see page 27), you can send the ball curving away from the goal (an outswinging corner) or in towards the goal (an inswinging corner). Both can be dangerous. An outswinger curves away from the goalkeeper and towards attackers running into the penalty area.

Corners are given when the ball leaves either end of the pitch and the defending team touched it last. The ball has to be placed inside the corner quadrant and opponents must retreat at least 9.1m. The corner taker has plenty of options, including passing the ball along the ground to a teammate making a run to the front of the penalty area, or hitting a high cross deep into the goal area.

Successful corners rely on both a good delivery and well-timed runs by attackers into the penalty area. Here, two attackers on the right are timing their runs into the box to meet the corner at just the right time. Another option is to play a short corner to the edge of the penalty area to catch the other team out.

Drop balls are used to restart the game after some stoppages. The referee stands between one player from each team and releases the ball. The players can challenge for the ball as soon as it touches the ground.

FIRST DEFENDER: the defender nearest to the corner kick, who is usually placed on the near post

Football terms

Fouls and free kicks

There is usually some physical contact in a game of football. However, when one team gains an unfair advantage by breaking a law, such as being caught offside, the referee will stop play by blowing his whistle and award a free kick to the opposing team.

Referees award two types of free kick – indirect and direct. A goalkeeper handling a backpass or a player causing dangerous play will result in an indirect free kick. Here the ball must be touched by one player before a second can shoot at goal. A direct free kick can be shot at goal and is awarded for fouls such as pushing, tripping or kicking an opponent.

This player has used an unfair amount of force to barge his opponent out of the way and almost send him sprawling to the floor. The referee will stop the game to award a free kick to the fouled player's team at the place where the offence occurred.

Some contact during a tackle is often inevitable, but if the player connects with an opponent before playing the ball then the referee will signal a foul.

A player who deliberately handles the ball or sticks out an arm to block its path is guilty of handball. The referee will award a free kick.

Tugging the shirt of an opponent to prevent their movement or laying your hands on an opponent's body to pull or hold them back are fouls.

Awarded a free kick, this alert player places the ball and is looking for opportunities to take a quick free kick. He can pass forwards to a teammate and start an attack before the other team can regroup.

A referee and his assistants try to get every decision correct, but they will not always be in the best position to judge a split second of action. Always accept the officials' decisions and never argue. Instead, retreat rapidly into a good defensive position in case your opponents take a quick free kick.

★ *Masterclass* ★

Cristiano Ronaldo
With his searing pace and trickery, Portuguese winger Cristiano Ronaldo often lures opponents into giving away free kicks for fouls. He is also expert at taking them. Thousands of hours of practice have given Ronaldo an array of free-kick shots, including fiercely struck shots that bend and dip on their way to goal.

As soon as a free kick is given against your side, retreat to at least 9.1m from the ball. If you fail to do so, the referee may show you a yellow card.

An attacking free kick usually sees a defensive wall of players positioned to guard much of the goal. The free kick taker may look to bend the ball up and over or around the edge of the wall towards the goal. Alternatively, he may choose to pass the ball to one side, bypassing the wall, for a teammate to have a clear strike on goal.

Football terms   **WALL**: a row of defenders protecting their goal against a free kick

Penalties

A foul or infringement by the defending team inside their penalty area, such as a deliberate handball, will see the referee award a penalty kick. This is a superb chance to score, with the ball placed just 11.1m from goal and only the goalkeeper to beat. Even so, many penalties are missed because of poor technique or an outstanding save.

A goalkeeper stands on the balls of his feet, ready to spring as the penalty is taken. A keeper can move along his goal line before the kick is taken, but must not move forwards.

A defender has badly fouled and brought down an attacker who was about to shoot inside the penalty area. The referee awards a penalty to the attacking team and may show the defender a red card.

Taking a penalty is an exercise in keeping calm and using good technique. Decide on the type of penalty you want to take before your run-up and stick to it. Make sure you get your body over the ball and strike it through the middle – this will help to keep the ball down and on target.

Carefully place the ball on the penalty spot, treading down any divots around the ball, and pace out your run-up. Try to shut out all distractions and focus on where you intend to aim the ball.

This penalty taker has used a firm sidefoot pass for control and aimed the ball into one of the corners – hard for any keeper to reach. Other players choose to hit the ball with an instep drive for power.

Penalty shootouts are used to decide the winner in some knockout competitions when the game has ended in a draw. They can provide thrilling, nerve-wracking viewing as each team takes alternate penalties. If the scores are level after five penalties each, pairs of penalties, one per side, are taken until one team misses and one team scores and wins.

Stay alert and do not turn away in disgust if your penalty is saved. The keeper may push the ball back out, giving you a second shot on goal.

PRO TIPS

This keeper has chosen the right direction to dive and makes a save. In a regular penalty kick, players can follow up, so the keeper will want to hold on to the ball. In a penalty shootout, no opponent can follow up with a second attempt on goal.

Players from both teams must stay outside the penalty area until the ball has been struck. They can then race into the area to either clear a rebound if they are on the defending side, or to try to score if they are on the attacking team.

Football terms   **RUN-UP:** the paces a player takes as he or she moves towards the ball to take a shot

Team tactics

Tactics are the way a team plays during a game – how the players try to defend and attack, where they are positioned and their specific roles. A coach is in charge of tactics and will look to catch out an opposing team by exploiting weaknesses such as slow or inexperienced full-backs or using his own team's strengths to their fullest.

Teams line up at the start of a game in rows of defenders, midfielders and attackers. This is called a formation. This 4-4-2 formation features two strikers playing in front of four midfielders.

4-4-2 formation

Even with the same formations, two teams can play quite differently by adopting different styles of play. Some teams use long, upfield passes to their strikers to launch quick attacks, while others prefer more patient build-up play, using lots of short passes to keep possession and probe for openings.

A team's defenders have moved up quickly and decisively in a straight line across the pitch to catch an opponent offside. This offside trap is used as a defensive tactic by some teams.

A single striker may be played upfront, using strength and skill to shield the ball and make lay-off passes to fellow attackers who play a short distance behind them.

3-5-2 formation

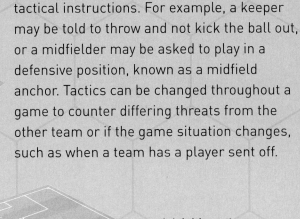

This is a popular formation as it can be set out as attack-minded or defensive. The wide midfielders in a 3-5-2 can push on when their team has the ball to provide lots of width in attack.

Individual players may be given specific tactical instructions. For example, a keeper may be told to throw and not kick the ball out, or a midfielder may be asked to play in a defensive position, known as a midfield anchor. Tactics can be changed throughout a game to counter differing threats from the other team or if the game situation changes, such as when a team has a player sent off.

4-4-1-1 formation

Popular with many teams, 4-4-1-1 sees four defenders and midfielders looking to feed a centre forward with a second striker playing in the hole behind him.

An attacker is substituted for a midfielder by a team's coach. Substitutions are a vital part of tactical play, allowing a coach to replace a tired or underperforming player or to reshape the team to be more attack- or defence-minded.

Sometimes, a team may choose one of its midfielders to mark a dangerous opponent, such as a playmaker who often sets up chances for strikers. The aim is to starve the player of time and space in which to create chances.

Read about football tactics and watch the analysis of games on TV to learn more about how teams play. If unsure of a tactic your team is adopting, always ask your coach to explain.

PRO TIPS

SUBSTITUTION: replacing one player on the team with another from the substitutes' bench

Football terms

Young players listen to instruction at a Juventus U12 women's training session at Juventus Centre, Vinovo, Italy.

Professional football

All talented young footballers dream of being paid to play for a professional club. As they progress through school, local and regional teams, young players may be signed to train and hone their skills in a professional club's youth system. Competition is fierce and only a tiny handful of young players will ever make the grade.

Supporters of Brazilian team Flamengo make a colourful spectacle during a match against Boa Vista. All over the world, fans flock to watch their club side play, devoting a lot of time and money to follow their team.

Football is played at professional level by clubs in every continent, but the powerhouse leagues containing the world's richest clubs are all found in Europe. These attract the cream of playing talent from Africa, Asia and the Americas, giving many top European club sides a truly international flavour.

An English Premier League game is a truly international affair. Here, Everton's English midfielder, Leon Osman, is crowded out by three Manchester City players – Ivorian Yaya Touré, Vincent Kompany from Belgium and Samir Nasri from France.

At its top end, professional football is a massive business. In 2011, for example, Real Madrid earned more than 430 million Euros while Barcelona pay Lionel Messi over 30 million Euros per season. Top players are wealthy and major celebrities, but fame and fortune dwindle rapidly outside the biggest leagues, with some clubs struggling to stay in business.

Professional football leagues exist for women in a number of countries, including Germany, North America (the Women's Professional Soccer league) and, from 2011, England (the Women's Super League). Here, Shannon Boxx (left) of the Los Angeles Sol and Yael Averbuch of the New Jersey Sky Blue chase the ball during a WPS game.

Cristiano Ronaldo and Kaka attack for Real Madrid, the club that broke the world transfer record to sign Kaka for £56 million in 2007 and again in 2009 to sign Ronaldo for £80 million.

A selection of shirts, scarves and other merchandise go on sale at a Chelsea FC stall. Sales of merchandise and tickets, along with sponsorship and the sale of TV rights, are key ways for a football club to earn money.

"My interest is in the collective success of the team, not individual glory."

Lionel Messi, Barcelona and Argentina

MERCHANDISE: souvenirs, clothing and other items bought by fans

Football terms

Major competitions

Football clubs compete in leagues (where teams play each other twice or more in a season) and knockout cup competitions both within their own country and involving clubs from abroad. These include the Copa Libertadores in South America and the UEFA Champions League in Europe.

El Hadji Diouf, playing for Glasgow Rangers moves away with the ball during his side's Scottish Cup match against fierce rivals, Celtic. First held in 1873-74, the competition has been dominated by these two teams with Celtic winning the trophy 38 times, five more than Rangers.

The Japanese J League began as a professional competition in 1993 and now features 18 teams. Kashima Antlers and Sanfrecce Hiroshima are the most successful clubs, with both winning eight league titles each.

Juventus striker Gonzalo Higuain shields the ball from Real Madrid's Raphael Varane during the 2017 UEFA Champions League Final. Real Madrid won 4-1 to secure a record 13th Champions League title. Juventus have won the competition twice and been runners-up a record seven times.

National teams also take part in continental competitions. These include the UEFA European Championship and the Asian Cup. The oldest continental competition, the Copa America for South American teams, began in 1916. The African Cup of Nations started out with just three teams in 1957, but now more than 50 take part. Countries also send men's and women's teams to compete at the Summer Olympics.

SAMUEL ETO'O

Cameroon's star striker, Samuel Eto'o is the African Cup of Nations' record goalscorer with 18 goals in six tournaments.

The FA Cup is the world's oldest surviving cup competition, starting all the way back in 1871-72. Arsenal (centre) are its most successful side. The club's wins in 2014, 2015 and 2017 brought its total to 13 triumphs.

Jailson of Brazilian club, Gremio, dribbles the ball during the 2017 Copa Libertadores Final against Argentinean side, Lanús. Gremio won the competition, after a gap of 22 years, to make it their third title.

Australia's Brett Holman (right) challenges Iraq's Qusai Munir during the 2011 Asian Cup. Australia first competed in Asian football in 2007, and in 2015 both hosted and won the tournament.

Egypt players hold the African Cup Nations trophy. The team has triumphed a record seven times, ahead of Cameroon with five wins, the latest in 2017.

The World Cup

Since its launch in 1930, the peak of football competition is the FIFA World Cup. Players in more than 200 national teams dream of qualifying for the 32-team tournament, which is held once every four years. Teams that reach the World Cup finals know they are just seven games away from lifting the famous trophy as world champions.

South African fans cheer on their team during the 2010 World Cup. The tournament was held in their country, and was the first time it had been hosted in Africa.

Iker Casillas holds the World Cup trophy in the air as his Spanish teammates celebrate winning the 2010 World Cup in front of more than 84,000 spectators.

Iceland's Björn Sigurdarson controls the ball during his country's 2-0 win over the Ukraine during qualifying for the 2018 World Cup. Both Iceland and Panama's appearance at the 2018 tournament held in Russia was their first.

Teams battle it out in qualifying competitions in their region to reach the finals. They are then split into eight groups, each with four teams. The top two sides in each group go into a knockout competition. The next three rounds of matches determine the two teams that will play in the final. Brazil is the most successful nation, winning five times, Italy and Germany have four wins. The German side has also finished in the top three at the tournament a record 12 times.

Germany's Linda Bresonik defends during her team's 11-0 win over Argentina. It remains a Women's World Cup record although Germany went close in 2015 with a 10-0 win over Ivory Coast.

The FIFA Women's World Cup began in 1991 and has helped to boost women's football. The 2015 tournament in Canada attracted 1.35 million fans and was won by the USA for the third time. The next competition will be held in France in 2019.

Diego Forlán controls the bouncing ball, shielding it from South Korean opponents during the 2010 World Cup. With five goals, Forlán was awarded the Golden Ball as the tournament's best player.

Thomas Müller congratulates his German team-mate, Mario Götze after he scored the winning goal in the 2014 World Cup Final versus Argentina. The tournament was held in Brazil and was the first time a European team had been crowned champions in South America.

EXTRA TIME: a period of extra play in some competitions when the scores are level after full time

Football terms

Football legends

Throughout football's history, certain players have amazed and dazzled with their skills, athleticism and daring. Here are some of the game's greatest legends and current leading stars.

Franz Beckenbauer

A superb defender for Bayern Munich and West Germany, Beckenbauer revolutionized the role of sweeper to stride into midfield and build attacks. He scored 14 times for his country, captained them to World Cup glory in 1974 and coached them to victory at the 1990 finals.

Lionel Messi

The gifted Argentinean attacker he spent all of his adult career at Barcelona where he has won nine La Liga titles and dazzled fans with his mazy dribbling and extraordinary goals. He, along with Ronaldo, are considered the best attackers on the planet.

Michel Platini

Part of a gifted French team of the late 1970s and 1980s, Platini was an excellent passer and a spectacular free-kick taker who scored regularly. Since 2007, he has been president of UEFA, the body that runs football in Europe.

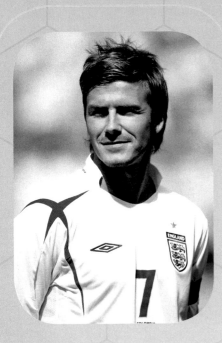

Hakan Sükür

This Turkish striker enjoyed three spells with Galatasaray and scored more than 350 times for various clubs. His 51 goals for the Turkish national team include the World Cup's fastest ever, scored after just 10.89 seconds when Turkey finished third at the 2006 World Cup.

Marta

Small at just 1.63m in height, yet packing a powerful shot, the Brazilian forward has been named World Player of the Year a record five times.

David Beckham

Beckham spent ten years at Manchester United, where his accurate passes and free-kick taking prowess helped the team to six Premier League titles and the 1999 UEFA Champions League. A move to Real Madrid, LA Galaxy and PSG followed with his retirement in 2013.

Manuel Neuer

A Champions League winner with Bayern Munich and World Cup winner with Germany, Neuer is an athletic goalkeeper who sometimes plays more like a defender. Appointed captain of Germany in 2016, he has won six German league titles.

George Best

Wayward but brilliant, George Best had spells with more than a dozen clubs, but is best known for his barnstorming displays for Manchester United. Capable of riding brutal tackles and swerving and dribbling through an entire defence, Best entertained millions of fans.

SWEEPER: a defender who plays behind the main line of defenders

Football terms

Iker Casillas

One of the finest keepers of the modern era, Casillas played over 700 game for Real Madrid before moving to Porto in 2015. Extremely agile, he was judged the best keeper at the 2010 World Cup which his side, Spain, won.

Ferenc Puskas

Packing a powerful shot, Puskas was the jewel in the crown of a Hungarian team that won the 1952 Olympics and crushed opponents with their attacking play. He won three European Cups with Real Madrid.

Pelé

Arguably the greatest footballer of all time, Pelé was certainly the game's finest all-round attacker, scoring 77 goals for Brazil and over 1,200 for Santos and his other clubs. The only player to win three World Cup winner's medals, Pelé remains a much-loved and respected figure in world football.

Cristiano Ronaldo

With blistering pace, swagger and tremendous skill, Ronaldo is a modern soccer superstar. He moved from Manchester United to Real Madrid in 2009 for whom he has scored over 400 goals at an astonishing rate of more than one per game. Crowned the world's best player in 2016 and 2017, he captained Portugal to win Euro 2016.

Eusébio

African football's first superstar, Eusébio moved from his native Mozambique to play for Benfica in 1960. He scored more than 450 goals for the club and top-scored at the 1966 World Cup with nine.

Diego Maradona

The only realistic rival to Pelé's crown as the best footballer, the stocky Argentinian was simply impossible to stop at times. He scored FIFA's goal of the century – a 60m dribble past many of the England team at the 1986 World Cup.

Gheorghe Hagi

Unpredictable and highly skilful, Gheorghe Hagi was Romania's finest player in the 1980s and 1990s, winning 125 caps and scoring 34 goals for his country. After spells with clubs including Real Madrid, Hagi helped the Turkish side Galatasaray win the 2000 UEFA Cup.

CAPS: the number of appearances made by a footballer for their national team

Football terms

Johan Cruyff

A truly gifted attacker, Cruyff scored 33 times in just 48 appearances for the Netherlands. Cruyff enjoyed great success at Ajax and Barcelona.

Zbigniew Boniek

The scorer of an awesome hat-trick (three goals) against Belgium in the 1982 World Cup, in which Poland finished third, Boniek was a hard-running, attacking midfielder. After seven seasons at Widzew Lodz, he joined Michel Platini at Juventus, winning Serie A titles and the 1985 European Cup.

Xavi Hernández

A master at unlocking defences, Xavi has spent his entire club career at Barcelona, where he has won six Spanish league titles and three Champions League crowns. Xavi has also won the 2008 European Championship and the 2010 World Cup with Spain.

Zinedine Zidane

Zidane played a key role as France swept to World Cup glory in 1998 and then became Euro 2000 champions. Sudden bursts of pace, a perfect first touch and excellent awareness allowed him to unlock defences with passes or runs. Zidane enjoyed spells at both Juventus and Real Madrid before retiring in 2006 and becoming Real Madrid manager 10 years later.

Kelly Smith

England's finest female footballer, Kelly Smith's goals and work rate helped to propel Arsenal Ladies FC to four league titles and three women's FA Cups. She has also won more 117 caps for England before retiring in 2014.

Birgit Prinz

A powerful player and lethal goalscorer, Prinz was the youngest player ever to appear in a World Cup final in 1995. She has since played more than 200 times for Germany.

Mia Hamm

One of the golden generation of American female footballers, Mia Hamm won World Cups and Olympic gold medals. She was the first female player to break the 100-goal international barrier in 1999, a testament to her ice-cool finishing and athletic, all-round play.

Landon Donovan

A Major League Soccer (MLS) superstar during his seasons at San Jose Earthquakes and LA Galaxy, Donovan has also played for Bayer Leverkusen and had short loan spells with Bayern Munich and Everton. Making his debut for the US team against Mexico in 2000, he has since become the US team's joint-leading scorer with Clint Dempsey with 57 goals.

Neymar Jr

An Olympic gold medallist with Brazil, Neymar shines with his explosive dribbling and goalscoring. He scored over 250 goals by the time he turned 25. He moved to Barcelona in 2013 and in 2017 switched to Paris Saint Germain for a world record transfer fee of over 220 million Euros.

Glossary

advantage
When a referee lets play continue after one of the laws of the game has been broken, giving the fouled-against team a benefit or advantage to continue an attack.

assistant referee
An official who assists the referee during the game, running up and down the sideline with a flag.

backheel
A short pass made with the back of the foot.

caps
The number of appearances made by a footballer for his or her national team.

chip
A pass lofted steeply into the air from a player to a teammate, or as a shot on goal.

cross
A pass sent from a wide position into the penalty area.

crossbar
The horizontal bar that connects the tops of the goal's two upright posts.

cushioning
Slowing the path of the ball using a part of the body, such as the foot, chest or head.

deflection
A sudden change in the direction of the ball after it has hit a player.

dribbling
Moving the ball under close control with a series of short kicks or taps.

extra time
A period of extra play in some competitions, when the scores are level after full time.

feint
Using a fake move of the body to send an opponent in the wrong direction or to put them off balance.

FIFA
Short for Fédération Internationale de Football Association, the international governing body of soccer.

first defender
The defender nearest to the corner kick, who is usually placed on the near post.

flexibility
The amount you can move your joints and body parts.

formation
The way in which a team lines up on the field in terms of defenders, midfielders and forwards.

free kick
A kick awarded to a team when the opposition breaks one of the game's laws.

goalside
Placing your body in between the goal and the ball or an opponent.

instep
The part of a player's foot where their boot laces lie.

intercepting
When one team makes a pass but an opponent gains control of the ball.

jockeying
A defensive technique of delaying an opposition player with the ball from passing or continuing an attack.

marking
Guarding a player to prevent him or her advancing the ball towards the goal, making an easy pass or getting the ball from a teammate.

merchandise
Souvenirs, clothing, match programmes and other items for sale, bought by fans of club or national teams.

obstruction
Blocking an opponent from reaching the ball without any attempt to reach the ball yourself.

opponent
A player from the other, opposing football team.

overlap
To make a run beyond a teammate down the side of the pitch.

overload
A situation in which the attacking team has more players in an area of the pitch than the defending team.

penalty
A kick awarded to a team when the opposition breaks one of the game's laws inside their own penalty area. Only the penalty taker and the goalkeeper are allowed inside the penalty area during the kick.

penalty area
The rectangular area, 40.2m wide, surrounding each goal.

penalty shootout
A method of deciding a drawn game by a series of penalties, taken from one end of the pitch.

possession
When one player or team has control of the football.

professional
Football in which the players are paid a full-time wage to play.

red card
Shown by a referee to send a player off the pitch as a punishment for a serious offence.

Serie A
The top Italian league championship.

set piece
A planned play or move that a team uses when a game is restarted with a free kick, penalty kick, corner kick, goal kick, throw-in or kick-off.

shielding
The technique of protecting the ball by placing your body between the ball and an opponent.

stamina
An athlete's ability to perform at or close to his or her peak performance for long periods.

substitution
Replacing one player on the team with another from the substitutes' bench.

sweeper
A defender who plays behind the main line of defenders, sweeping up any attacks that break through the defensive line.

swerve
To bend the path of the ball. A swerve is made by striking the ball with one side of the foot so that it spins in a certain direction.

tactics
Methods of play used in an attempt to outwit and beat an opposition team.

through ball
A pass made to a teammate behind the other team's defence.

UEFA
Short for Union of European Football Associations, the governing body of football in Europe.

wall
A row of defenders protecting their goal against a free kick.

warm-up
The routine of stretches and gentle exercises performed by players to prepare their bodies before training or a match.

yellow card
Shown by a referee to warn a player who has committed an offence.

zonal marking
When each defending player guards a particular area of the pitch.

Websites

www.fifa.com/en/index.html
The official website of the organization that runs world football. The website contains details of qualifying and performances in leading tournaments, plus profiles of many leading teams and players.

www.uefa.com
The homepage of the Union of European Football Associations, the organization that runs the European Championship as well as the Champions League.

http://news.bbc.co.uk/sport1/hi/ football/skills/default.stm
A collection of videos and diagrams showing ways to improve and perfect key football skills.

www.planetworldcup.com/ index.html
A website devoted to the FIFA World Cup, packed with facts, statistics, stories and profiles of the tournament's top players.

www.premierleague.com
The official website of the English Premier League contains details of fixtures, results and many features on teams and players.

www.thefa.com/ football-rules-governance
Download the latest laws of the game at this webpage from the Football Association.

www.mlssoccer.com
The official website of Major League Soccer, the leading male soccer competition in the United States.

Index

Picture credits

The Publisher would like to thank the following for permission to reproduce their material. Every care has been taken to trace copyright holders.

t = top; b = bottom; c = centre; l = left; r = right

Cover Getty/Dmytro Aksonov, background image Shutterstock; Page 6bl Bongarts/Getty Images, 6-7c Getty Images, 7bl Getty Images, 7tr AFP/Getty Images, 8 Getty Images, 15tr Getty Images, 17tr The FA via Getty Images, 19bl Bongarts/Getty Images, 19br AFP/Getty Images, 21br Getty Images, 23tr AFP/Getty Images, 26bl AFP/Getty Images, 27tr AFP/Getty Images, 29tr AFP/Getty Images, 30bl Bongarts/Getty Images, 34bl Bongarts/Getty Images, 37tl Getty Images, 44bl The FA via Getty Images, 45tr Getty Images, 50t Joachim Ladefoged/VII/Corbis, 50cr LatinContent/Getty Images, 50b Getty/Valerio Pennicino - Juventus FC, 51tl Getty Images, 51bl Getty Images, 51r MLS via Getty Images, 52cl AFP/Getty Images, 52tr Getty Images, 52b Shutterstock/Chris Ricco, 53tl AFP/Getty Images, 53tc Getty Images, 53tr Getty/Amilcar Orfali/Stringer, 53b AFP/Getty Images, 53br AFP/Getty Images, 54cl AFP/Getty Images, 54b Shutterstock/ katatonia88, 54-55 Getty Images, 54-55b AFP/Getty Images, 55tr AFP/Getty Images, 55br Shutterstock/AGIF, 56bl Bob Thomas/Getty Images, 56r AFP/Getty Images, 57tl WireImage/ Getty Images, 57tr AFP/Getty Images, 57br Getty Images, 58tl AFP/Getty Images, 58tr AFP/Getty Images, 58b Time & Life Pictures/Getty Images, 59t Shutterstock/Marcos Mesa Sam Wordley, 59cr Getty Images, 59b Bob Thomas/Getty Images, 60tl AFP/Getty Images, 60tr Bob Thomas/Getty Images, 60b AFP/Getty Images, 61l Getty Images, 61b Shutterstock/ AGIF, 61tr Bongarts/Getty Images.